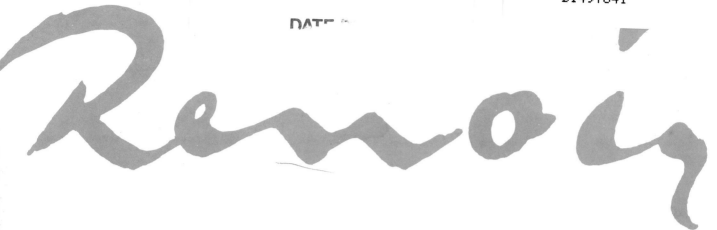

NANCY NUNHEAD

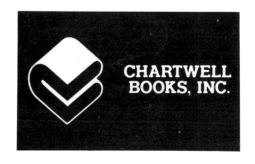

CHARTWELL
BOOKS, INC.

Published by
CHARTWELL BOOKS, INC.
A Division of BOOK SALES, INC.
110 Enterprise Avenue
Secaucus, New Jersey 07094

Produced by
Brompton Books Corp.
15 Sherwood Place
Greenwich, CT 06830

ISBN 1-55521-765-6

Printed in Hong Kong

LIST OF PLATES

Lise with a Parasol	4	*The Seine at Argenteuil*	26
Gabrielle and Jean	9	*Copy of Delacroix's 'Jewish Wedding'*	28
William Sisley	10	*Portrait of Madame Chocquet*	29
Potted Plants	11	*The Ball at the Moulin de la Galette*	30
The Pont des Arts	12	*The Skiff*	32
Nymph by a Stream	14	*The Luncheon of the Boating Party*	34
La Grenouillère	16	*Venice: Piazza San Marco*	36
Odalisque: Woman of Algiers	18	*Rocky Crags, l'Estaque*	38
Claude Monet Reading	20	*Dance at Bougival*	39
Parisiennes in Algerian Dress	21	*The Children's Afternoon at Wargemont*	40
Monet Painting in his Garden at Argenteuil	22	*Claude Renoir Playing*	42
La Loge	24	*The Umbrellas*	43
Dancer	25	*Acknowledgments*	44

PIERRE-AUGUSTE RENOIR

1841–1919

The works of all the Impressionist painters are well-known and frequently reproduced, but perhaps none are better-loved than those of Pierre-Auguste Renoir. His images of contented family life being conducted in sun-filled gardens seem to conjure for the modern spectator a lost Eden. And yet what we see is not some objective vision of 19th-century life but the embodiment of Renoir's own nostalgic longings. It is impossible fully to understand Renoir's art without being aware of this. Moreover other factors are of almost equal importance, for example the influence of biographers with a vested interest in promoting a particular interpretation of Renoir's art, such as his dealer Ambroise Vollard or his son Jean Renoir.

Renoir was born in Limoges on 25 February 1841, the sixth child of Léonard Renoir and his wife Marguerite Merlet. In 1844 Léonard Renoir moved his family to Paris where he earned a living as a tailor. Pierre-Auguste left school at 13, in 1854, and joined the porcelain manufacturers Lévy frères as a porcelain painter. His precocious talent for his work is recorded and perhaps from this time dates his lifelong respect for craft skills and his mistrust of mechanization. It was this latter development which saw Lévy frères go bankrupt in 1858: other manufacturers used mechanical processes to decorate porcelain much more cheaply than hand painters could. Without a job Renoir took what work he could find decorating fans and blinds.

In January 1860 Renoir obtained permission to copy works in the Louvre, a practice he was to pursue for the next four years. His taste was for Rococo works of the 18th century, such as those by Boucher, Watteau, Fragonard, and Lancret. A particular favorite is supposed to have been Boucher's *Bath of Diana*; although he was later to make several 'bather' paintings, at this date it seems to have been Boucher's frothy handling of the paint and his light tonality which attracted Renoir.

Perhaps inspired by his encounters with 'fine art', Renoir enrolled in 1861 in the Paris studio of Marie-Gabriel-Charles Gleyre, a Swiss teacher who offered modestly priced models and free tuition. He had had limited success at the Salon with works which were polished in execution but Romantic in mood; the Salon juries although they appreciated the former preferred classical subjects. As a young man Gleyre had met the English landscape painter Richard Parkes Bonington and this perhaps inspired him to practice this genre and to encourage his pupils to do likewise. Gleyre charged students 10 francs a month to cover models' fees and rent but accepted no money for tuition. Renoir seems to have liked and respected Gleyre and still referred to himself as a 'pupil of Gleyre' long after Gleyre's death.

LISE WITH A PARASOL, 1867
Oil on canvas, 72¼×45¼ inches (184×115 cm)
Folkwang Museum, Essen

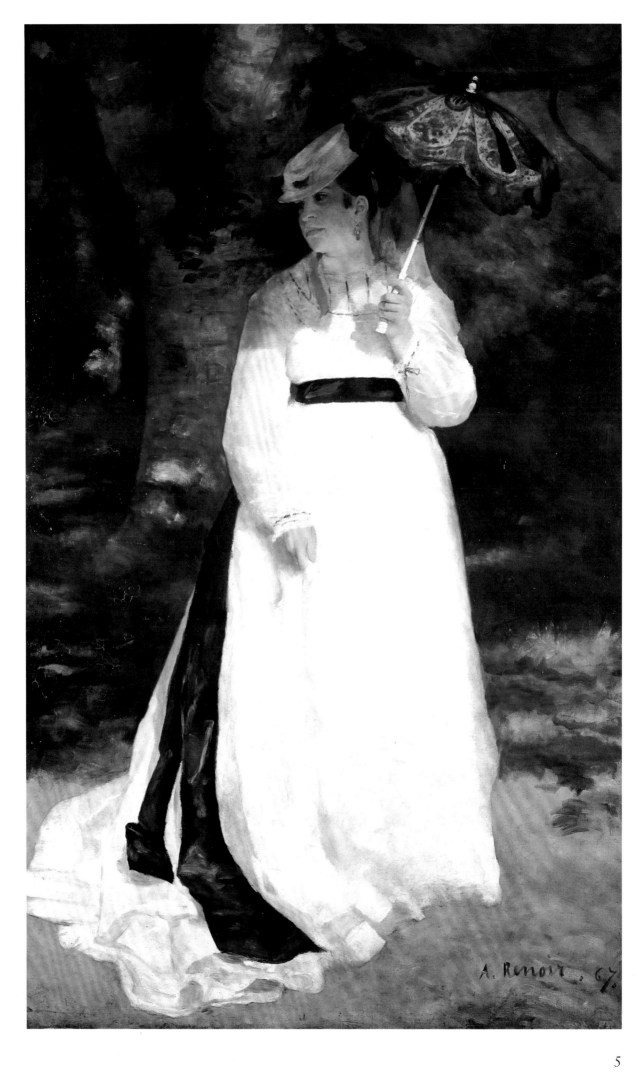

Two lessons he learnt then were to stay with Renoir: the importance of drawing as the basis of painting and the need to work on landscape painting in the open air.

As well as working at Gleyre's Renoir enrolled in 1862 for two years at the Ecole des Beaux-Arts. This decision reflects Renoir's desire to succeed as a painter; for any painter to succeed he (or, very occasionally, she) had to exhibit at the annual Salon, a huge exhibition whose jury was composed chiefly of members and professors of the Ecole des Beaux-Arts. Renoir may have submitted a work in 1863 but, if so, it was rejected along with an unprecedentedly large number of other works. This led to the Emperor Napoleon III sanctioning an alternative exhibition, the Salon des Refusés, for all the unsuccessful applicants to the Salon. Although many artists withdrew from this exhibition because of the fear of stigma at being associated with refusal, it did provide a model of sorts for other alternative exhibitions such as the Impressionist exhibitions from 1874 to 1886.

Renoir had his first Salon success the next year when he had a huge painting based on Victor Hugo's novel *Notre Dame de Paris* accepted, but he seems to have destroyed this work in dissatisfaction. Although Renoir was to continue to submit to the Salon for many years he never again sent such 'grandes machines,' as huge paintings with literary or historical subjects were called. In 1865 he sent a portrait of William Sisley, father of his friend the painter Alfred Sisley, and such relatively modestly proportioned and informal works became typical of his Salon submissions.

Alfred Sisley had been one of Renoir's fellow pupils at Gleyre's along with Claude Monet and Frédéric Bazille. Other painters he met at this time inluded Camille Pissarro and Paul Cézanne, who had attended the Académie Suisse, run on similar lines to Gleyre's. Thus by 1863 the core of the future Impressionist group was in existence. Some of the ideas that were to unite them were explored by Renoir, Bazille, Sisley, and Monet on a painting trip they took to Chailly in the Forest of Fontainebleau during Easter 1863. Although they worked in the open air, in the manner recommended by their master Gleyre and by Barbizon painters such as Millet and Corot, the works produced were not considered by them suitable to be exhibited as finished paintings. Rather they formed the basis of larger studio-produced works, with figures and other details added, acting as aide-memoires of such natural and ephemeral effects as sunlight. It was many years before Renoir executed paintings which he considered worthy of exhibition completely in the open air.

The increasing practice artists such as Monet and Renoir made of working in the open air was greatly facilitated by advances in artists' materials. By the 1860s ready-mixed paint in collapsible metal tubes was available as were lightweight, easily portable sketching easels. Renoir painted Monet using just such an easel in *Monet Painting in his Garden at Argenteuil* (1873). Such materials would have been crucial to Monet and Renoir when they worked together in the summer of 1869 painting at Le Grenouillère, a bathing and boating establishment on the Seine. Although Monet's letters of the time suggest that these paintings, including Renoir's *La Grenouillère*, were just sketches for larger finished works they both proposed to make later, they have been signed, suggesting the artists' satisfaction with them. Certainly compared with his other early landscapes, Renoir's paintings at La Grenouillère are revolutionary in their use of color, handling of paint, and apparent spontaneity of composition. The choppy brushwork is used to indicate very immediate effects of sunlight through foliage and across the rippling surface of the water. The color is remarkably different from the restricted palette of earth colors he had used for earlier, studio-produced landscapes and is remarkable both for its brightness and lightness, produced by mixing his colors with white, emulating the color effects of the 18th-century painters he admired. The composition, although no doubt carefully thought out, gives an appearance of spontaneity in the way elements such as the boats are cut off apparently arbitrarily.

By the early 1870s Renoir was having some measure of success. He had two works accepted for the 1870 Salon and in 1872 the dealer Paul Durand-Ruel whom Monet had introduced to him and who was to be an important early promoter of the Impressionists, bought one of his works. But it was perhaps his failure to have a work accepted at the 1873 Salon which led Renoir to join a group of other disaffected young painters in setting up the first Impressionist exhibition. Again a Salon des Refusés was held in 1873, but some felt something different was required. In December 1873 Renoir, Monet, Pissarro, Berthe Morisot, Sisley, and Degas, among others, registered themselves as a joint stock company for the purpose of staging an exhibition of their work. A major impetus for all of them, especially for Pissarro and Paul Cézanne who had been notably unsuccessful in their submissions to the Salon, was the need to find new markets for their work, especially as Durand-Ruel's early enthusiasm for their work saw him in financial difficulties by 1874.

The exhibition, which was open from 15 April to 15 May 1874 with long opening hours to encourage sales, included seven works by Renoir, including *La Loge*. It was held in a studio in the boulevard des Capucines formerly occupied by the photographer Nadar, and the flock wallpaper and mixture of natural and gaslight was thought to approximate conditions under which works would be seen in the average household. A major difference from the presentation of works at the Salon was that the exhibits were hung mostly on one level so that none was displayed too disadvantageously. Despite the presentation of the exhibition as a failure, it was visited by 3500 during the month it was open. Although one critic, Louis Leroy, in discussing Monet's *Impression: Sunrise*, used the term 'impressionist' derogatively, many critics found something positive to say about the works on display.

Despite the number of visitors business was not brisk and at the close of the exhibition each exhibitor was left owing 185 francs 50 centimes. To help clear their debts and to generate some more publicity, Monet, Renoir, Morisot, and Sisley held an auction of their work in March 1875. Renoir sold 20 paintings for 2251 francs, some for as little as 50 francs. He did succeed, however, in securing two new commissions. One from Victor Chocquet, a civil servant who was an early enthusiast for the Impressionsts, for a portrait of his wife Caroline, the other from the industrialist Jean Dollfuss who had Renoir copy Delacroix's *Jewish Wedding*, a painting in the Louvre. This latter work reveals the extent to which Renoir could adapt his style when economic pressures obliged him to. By the time of the second Impressionist exhibition of 1876 nine of Renoir's exhibited works were listed a loans. Although exhibiting works as 'already sold' was a device used by several of the Impressionists to stimulate the desire for their work it does suggest that Renoir was beginning to create a market for his work.

Perhaps encouraged by these successes Renoir began a large-scale work in the summer of 1876. Its subject was the Moulin de la Galette, a dance hall in Montmartre which still retained a rustic atmosphere in the 1870s. Renoir probably worked on a sketch or sketches in the open air and produced the large-scale version in his studio, but he invests it with many of the qualities of high tone and fleeting light effects he had captured in his on-the-spot studies. The painting, *The Ball at the Moulin de la Galette*, showed many of his friends sitting and dancing in the dance-hall garden and it was shown at the third Impressionist exhibition in 1877. During that exhibition a journal, *L'Impressioniste*, was produced, mainly written by Renoir's biographer Georges Rivière. He wrote approvingly of the *Ball at the Moulin de la Galette*:

Certainly M Renoir has a right to be proud of his *Ball* . . . It is a page of history, a precious moment of Parisian life depicted with rigorous exactitude. Nobody before had thought of capturing some aspect of daily life in a canvas of such large dimensions . . . He has attempted to produce a contemporary note and he has found it.

What Renoir had done was to realize a longstanding ambition of many writers and painters of the Realist and Naturalist traditions in creating a work which captured the particualr qualities of contemporary life and presented them on scale usually reserved for historical, allegorical, or literary subjects.

The late 1870s saw a greater measure of official recognition come Renoir's way. He had works accepted at both the 1879 and 1880 Salons. A law prevented exhibitors at the Impressionist exhibitions from showing at the Salon and in both 1878 and 1881 Renoir chose to exhibit at the Salon rather than at the fourth and fifth Impressionist shows. His motives were largely financial, as his fellow Impressionists such as Pissarro understood. For him to succeed he had to exhibit at the Salon and to keep doing so. None the less as an excuse for not joining the other Impressionists in 1881 he remarked to Paul Durand-Ruel:

For me to exhibit with Pissarro, Gauguin, and Guillaumin would be like exhibiting with any socialist . . .

During 1880 Durand-Ruel had spent 16, 000 francs on Renoir's paintings and Renoir took the opportunity of this financial security to travel, first to North Africa, then to Italy. The first trip to Algeria in March and April 1881 confirmed many of his interests of the past 10 or 15 years. Since French colonization of North Africa the sights and especially the women of North Africa had become popular as emblems of exoticism as Renoir's *Parisiennes in Algenian Dress* (1872), exhibited at the 1872 Salon, clearly demonstrates. A far more significant influence on Renoir's art in the 1880s was his trip to Italy from October 1881 to March 1882.

What he saw in Italy that so moved him were the classical Roman frescoes, some from Pompeii, which he saw in Naples, and Raphael's decorations of the Villa Farnesina in Rome. What he found in these works were answers to some of the questions he was asking himself about the limitations of impressionism. One of the main objectives of the impressionist style had been the accurate analysis and recording of effects of light and color reflexions on objects in the open air. But as Renoir came increasingly to realize, this automatic or objective recording of ephemeral effects was an unattainable goal, as it relied on the artist attempting to translate what were, to start with, his own subjective impressions into paint. The picture surface was in danger of breakdown. What was needed to prevent this was a new approach based on drawing providing an underlying structure. This approach had been recommended by his master Gleyre and it was perfectly exemplified by Raphael and the Roman artists of Pompeii.

A further impetus to Renoir finding a new and potentially lucrative idiom was increasing family responsiblities. In 1879 he had met a young woman from northeastern France called Aline Charigot. Although they did not marry until 1890 their first son, Pierre, was born in 1885. If Renoir's motives were financial he was not at first successful. His first essays in the new style were *The Children's Afternoon in Wargemont* and the *Bathers*. The latter was based on a classicizing 17th-century bas-relief in the gardens of the Palace of Versailles and remained unsold for some time after it was exhibited in May 1887. The change in Renoir's style is hightlighted by *The Umbrellas*, a painting begun in 1881 but not completed until 1886; while the righthand side is in the older impressionist mode, with soft broken brushwork and high tonality, the left side is much smoother in finish and more somber in tonality.

But the disapproval of former enthusiasts for his impressionist style had the happy converse of increasing Salon acceptablity. As well as looking for a new sense of structure in his paintings Renoir was increasingly to concentrate on the female nude, the archetypal classical and therefore favored Salon subject. Renoir's decision to exhibit solely at the Salon was due in part to his suspicions about what had happened to the Impressionist exhibitions. He came increasingly to feel that they were being usurped by artists whose views did not accord (artistically in the case of Gauguin, politically in the case of Pissarro) with his own. Although he could not prevent Durand-Ruel from exhibiting 27 of his works the dealer owned in the 1882 show, Renoir did not exhibit at the eighth and final Impressionist exhibition of 1886.

The 1880s as well as seeing a change in his practice, were years of increasing prosperity for Renoir. This is reflected in the scenes of comfortable bourgeois life, both his own and his patrons', which he increasingly preferred to paint. Renoir has been much criticized for his misogyny and for his reactionary political views. While it is true that many of his statements were anti-Semitic and that he was anti-Dreyfus, his views were not unusual in late 19th-century France and he did cultivate and socialize with his Jewish patrons. His attitude to women is more complex and difficult. Although he respected and greatly admired the work of Berthe Morisot, his view of women was that they were better when uneducated and confined to rearing children. This view is part of his general belief in a hierarchical society with everyone knowing their correct place and is certainly reflected in the way he presents women in his paintings, either as objects (of beauty or sexual desirability) or in confined domestic roles.

From the 1890s until his death in 1919 Renoir certainly had a supply of ready subjects for his domestic scenes. His first son, Pierre, was born in 1885, followed by Jean, later celebrated as a film director, in 1894, and Claude, known as Coco, in 1901. In 1896 a cousin of Mme Renoir, Gabrielle Renard, joined the household to help with the children. Renoir painted her many times on her own or with one or more of his sons. His final years were plagued by ill health and disability. From his fifties he had been afflicted by arthritis and this was compounded by rheumatism and the partial atrophy of a nerve in his left eye. None the less Renoir's final years were highly prosperous. His work was skillfully promoted by the dealer Ambroise Vollard whom he had met in the 1890s. In 1907-08 Renoir was able to build himself a house and studio at Cagnes in the south of France which has a mild, dry climate supposedly beneficial to rheumatism. For the last few years of his life he was confined to a wheelchair and had to have his brushes strapped to his hands, which may account for the rather loose brushwork in his final paintings. Renoir died in Cagnes, aged 78, on December 3rd, 1919; of the major Impressionist painters only Monet outlived him to enjoy even greater acclaim.

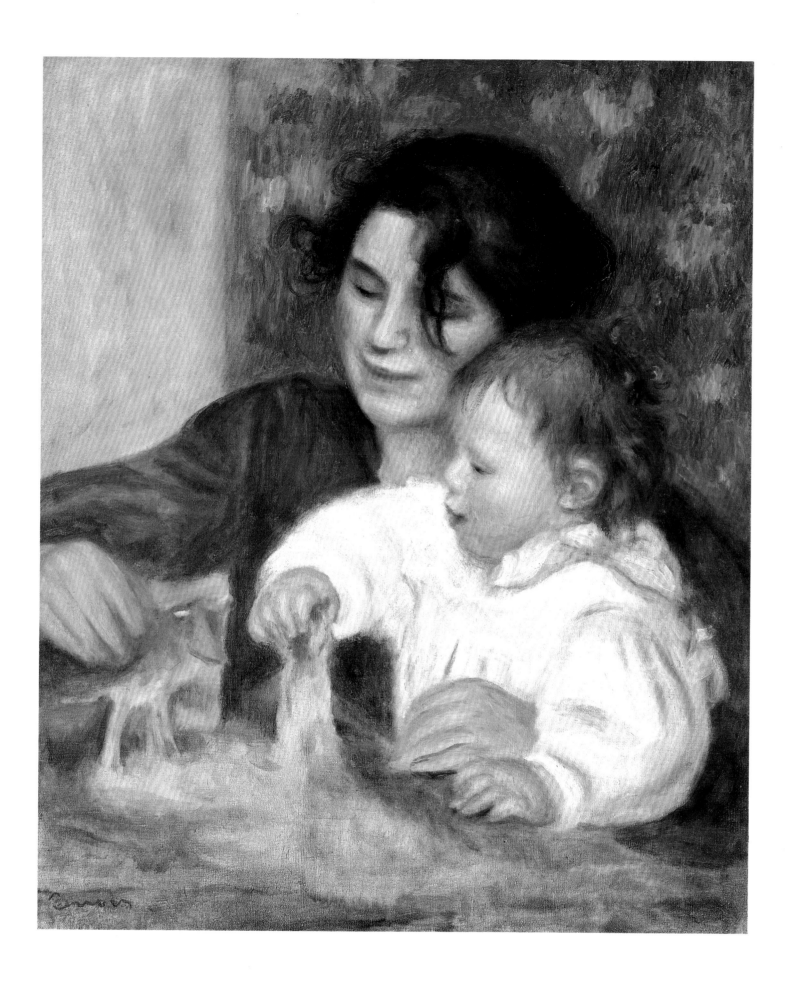

GABRIELLE AND JEAN, c. 1895
Oil on canvas, 25½×21¼ inches (65×54 cm)
Musée de l'Orangerie, Paris

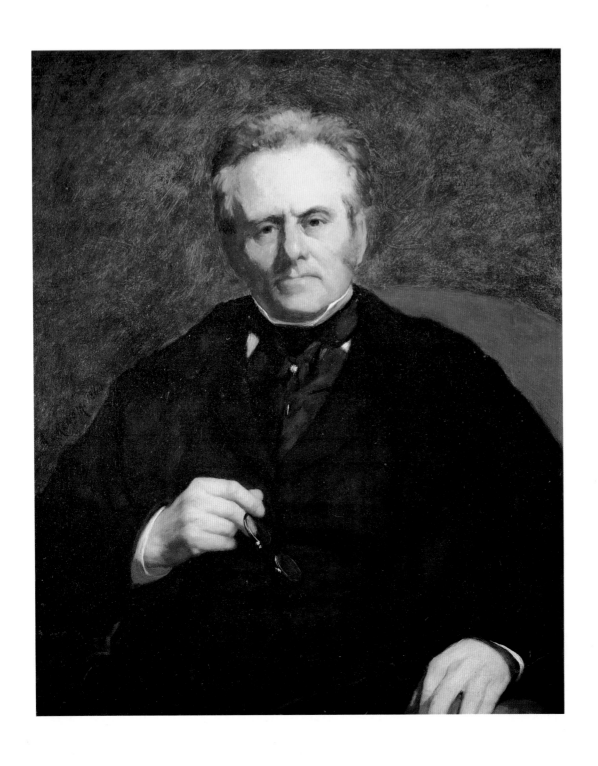

Above:
WILLIAM SISLEY, 1864
Oil on canvas, 32½×25¾ inches (81.5×65.5 cm)
Muséed'Orsay, Paris

Facing page
POTTED PLANTS, 1864
Oil on canvas, 51⅙×37¾ inches (130×96 cm)
Oskar Reinhart Collection 'Am Römerholz,' Winterthur

10

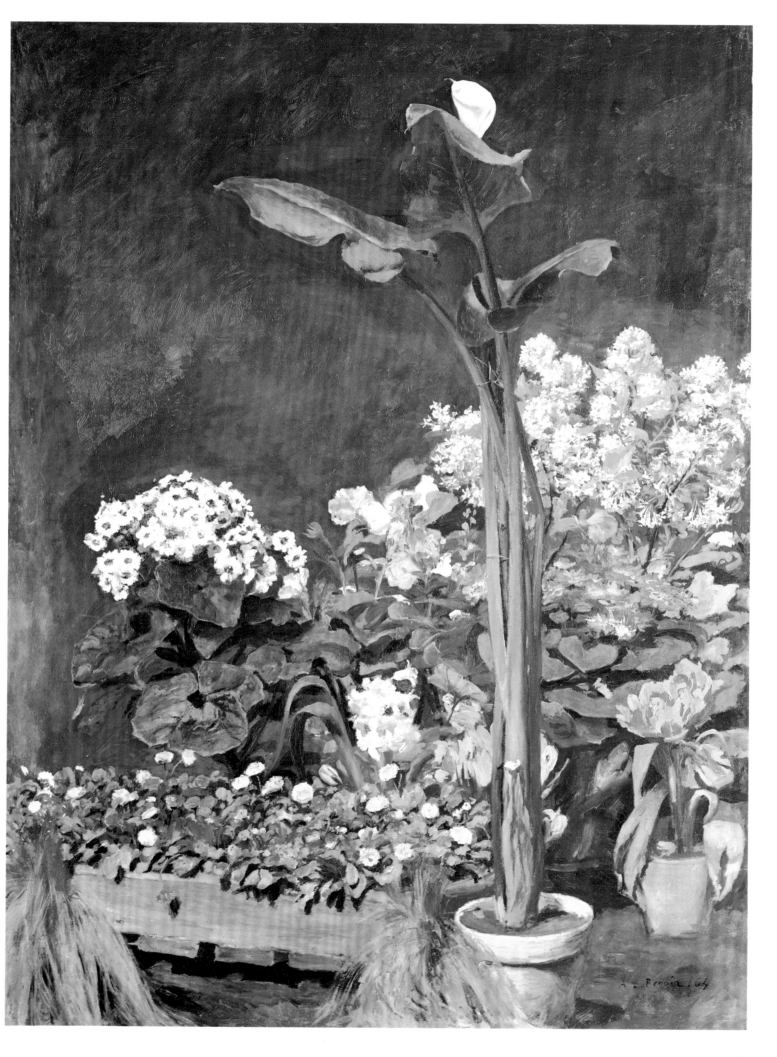

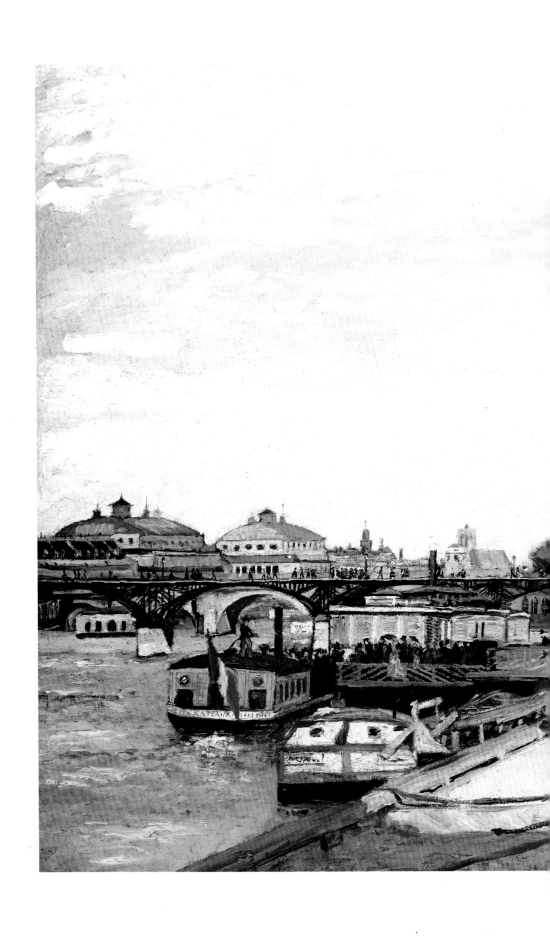

THE PONT DES ARTS, 1867
Oil on canvas, 24½×40½ inches (62.2×102.9cm)
The Norton Simon Foundation, Pasadena, California

12

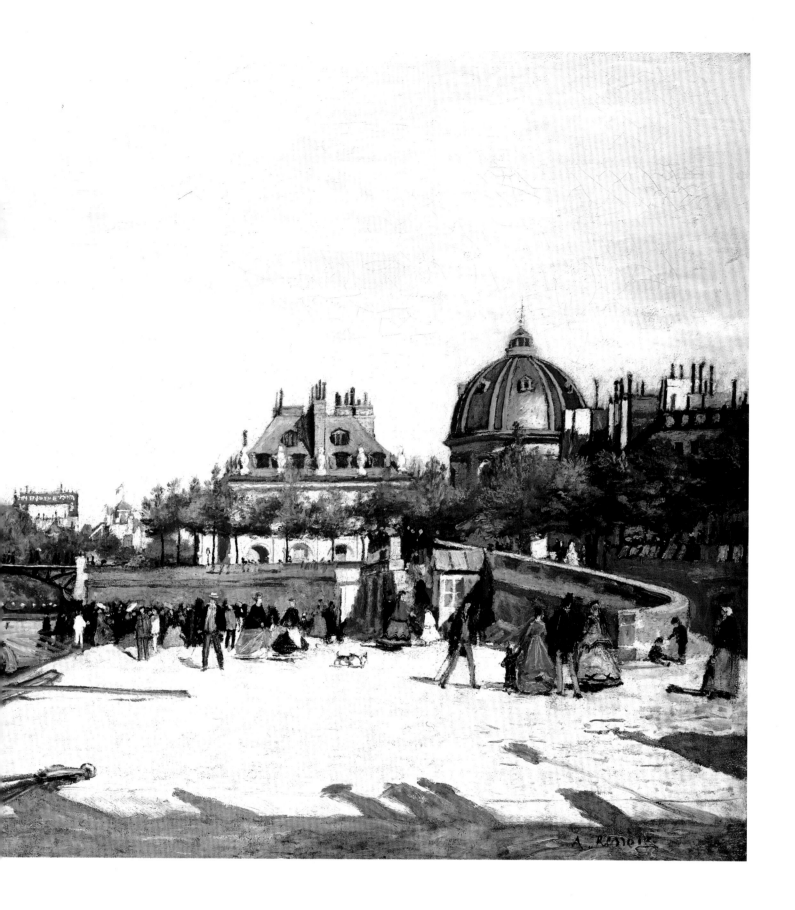

NYMPH BY A STREAM, c. 1869
Oil on canvas, 26⅜×48¾ inches (67×124 cm)
National Gallery, London

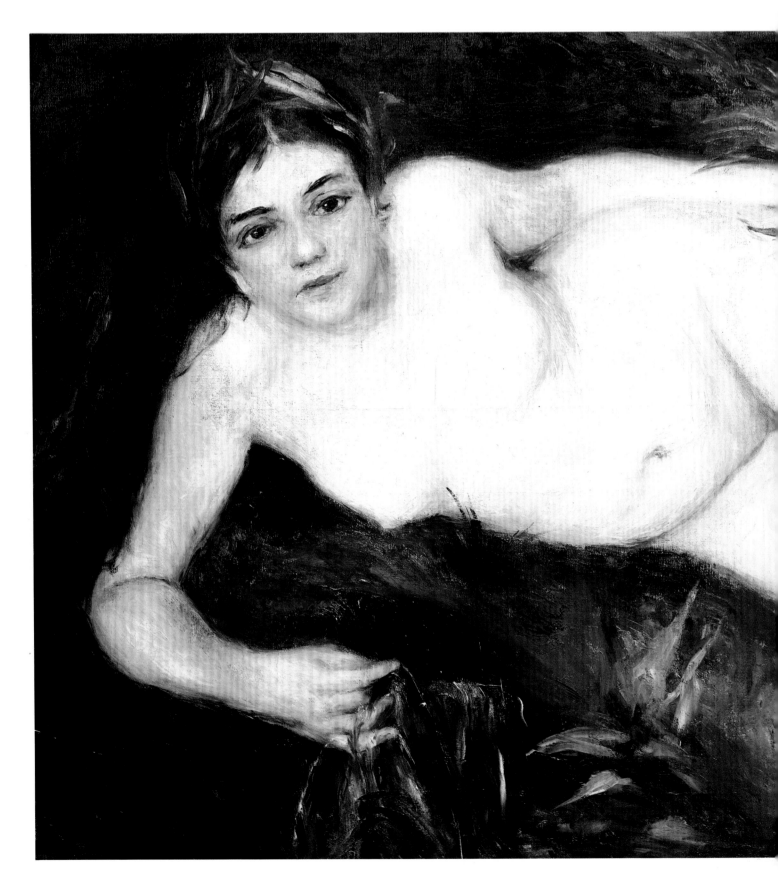

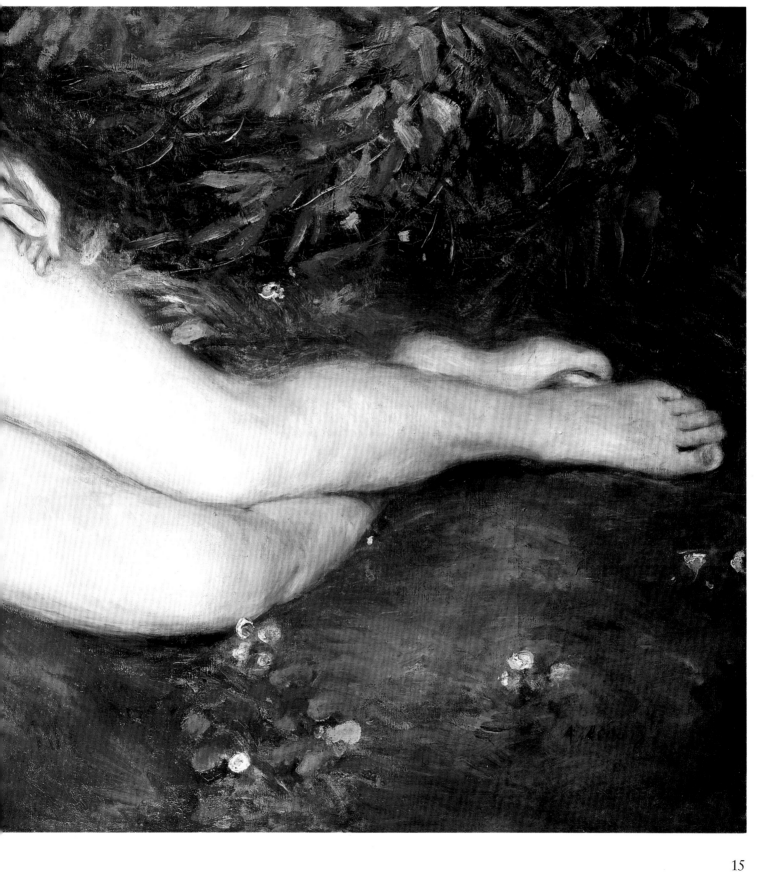

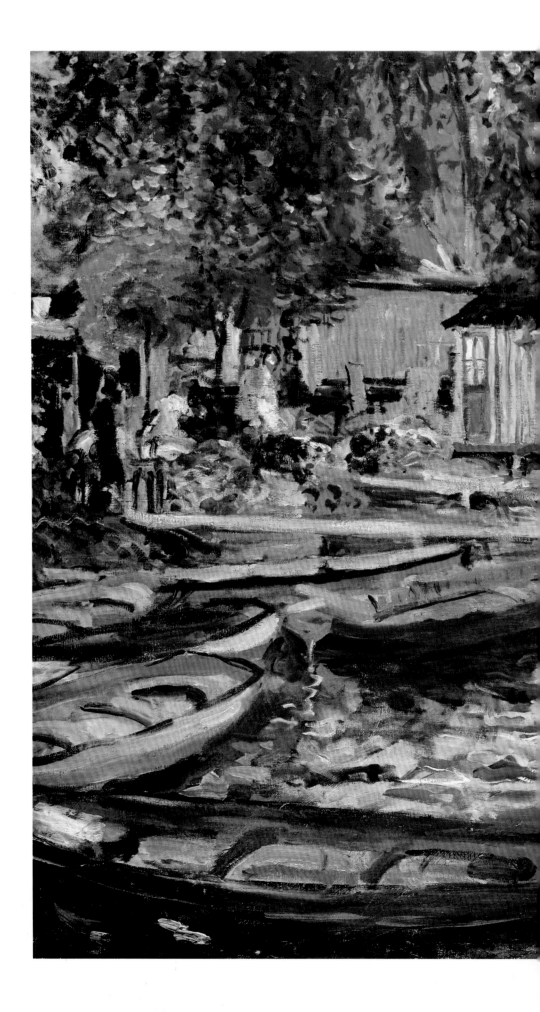

La Grenouillère, 1869
Oil on canvas, 25½×36⅝ inches (65×93 cm)
Oskar Reinhart Collection 'Am Römerholz', Winterthur

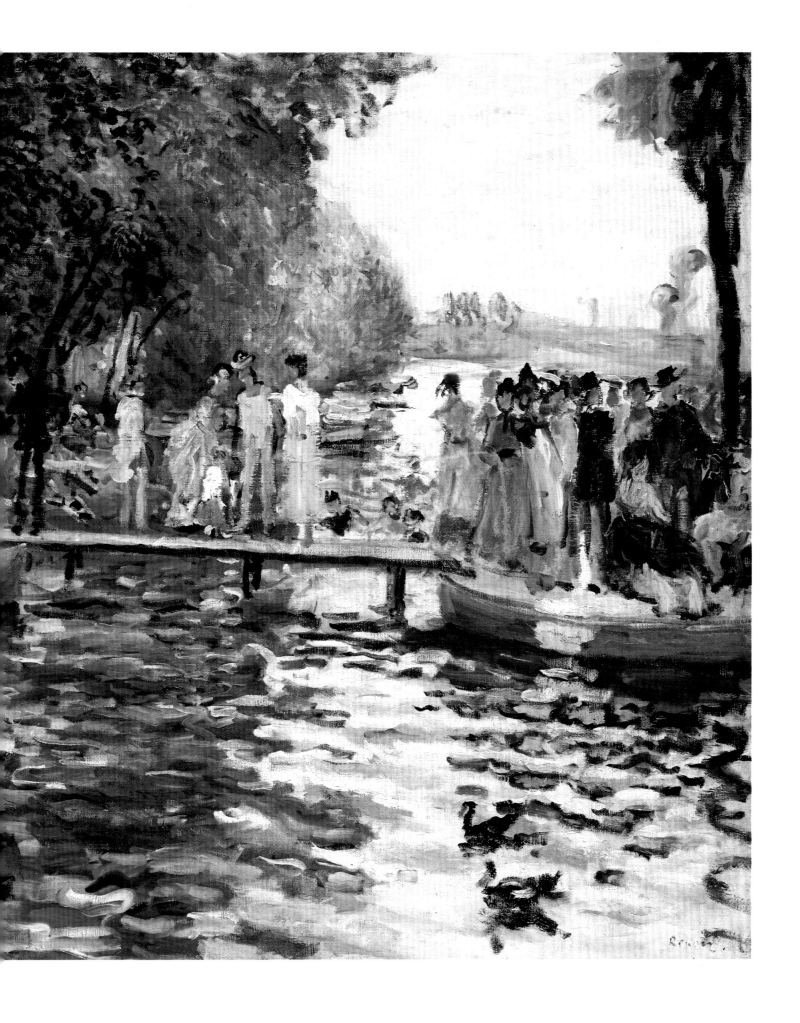

ODALISQUE: WOMAN OF ALGIERS, 1870
Oil on canvas, 27¼×48¼ inches (69.2×122.6 cm)
National Gallery of Art, Washington DC, Chester Dale Collection

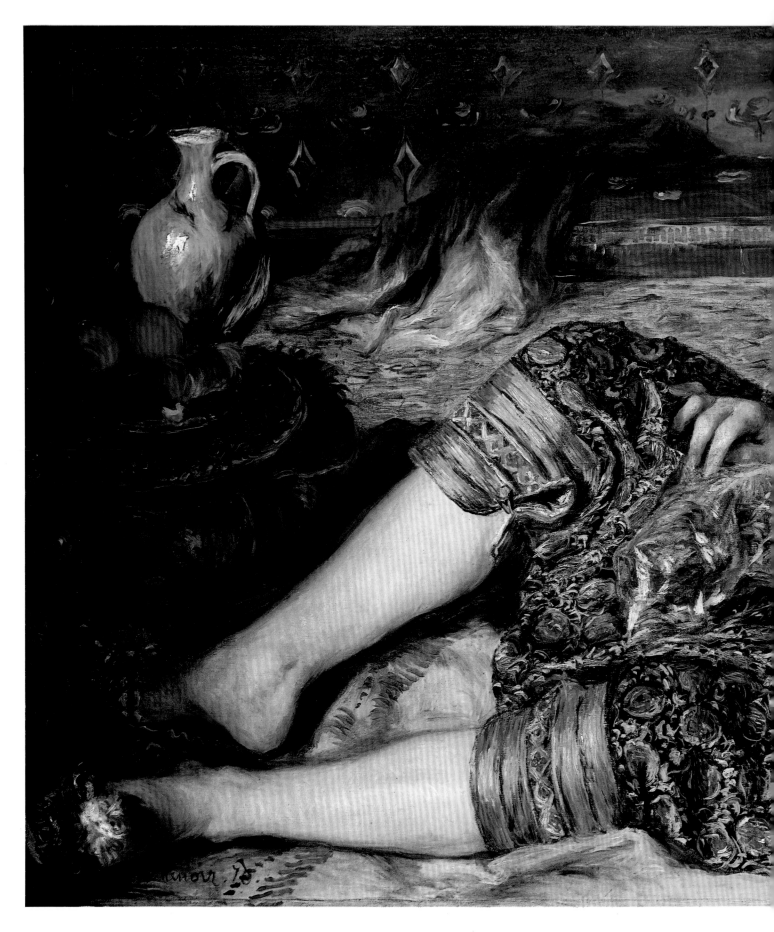

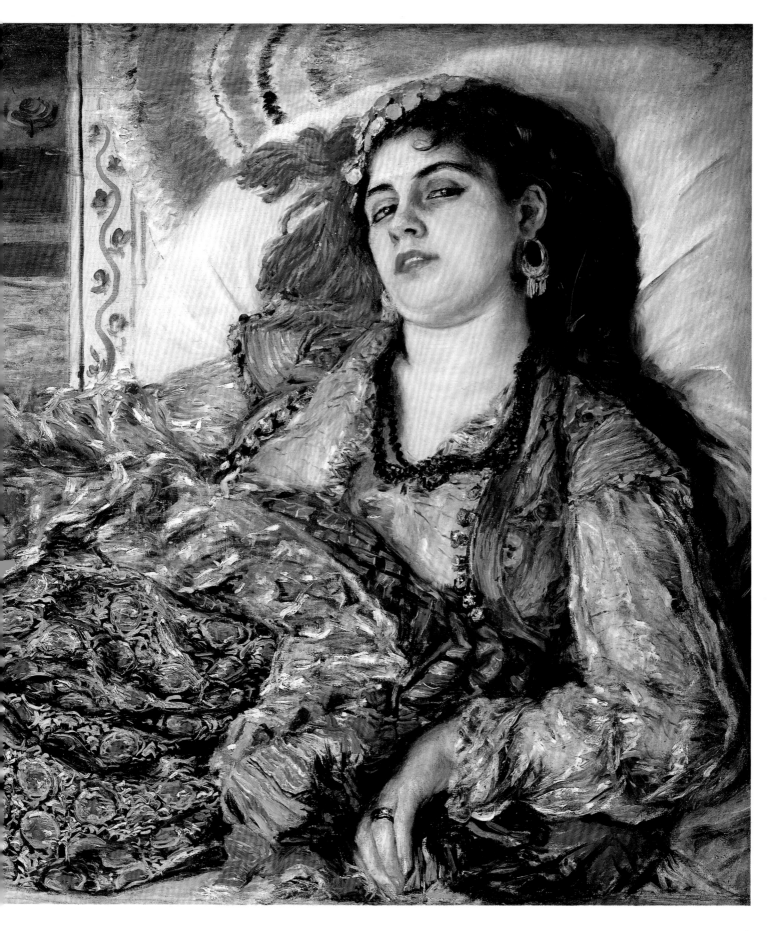

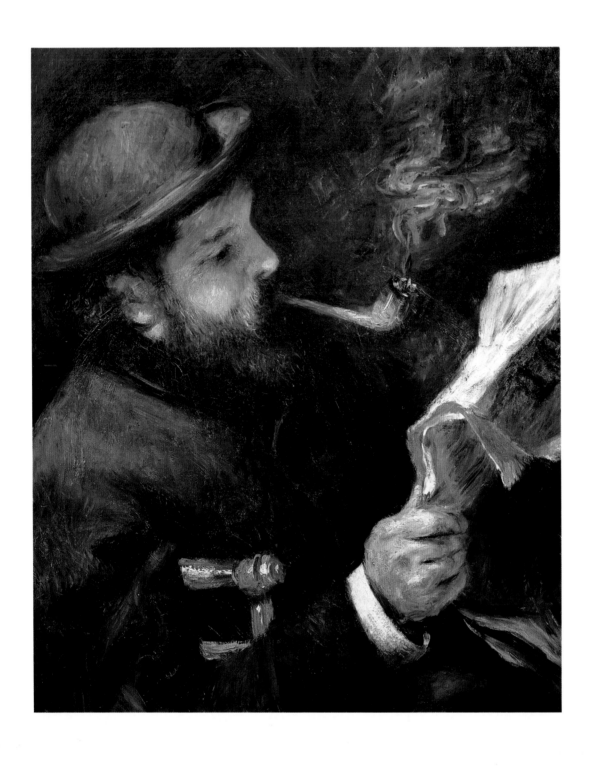

Above:
CLAUDE MONET READING, 1872
Oil on canvas, 24×19⅝ inches (61×50 cm)
Musée Marmottan, Paris

Facing page:
PARISIENNES IN ALGERIAN DRESS, 1872
Oil on canvas, 61¾×51½ inches (157×131 cm)
National Museum of Western Art, Tokyo,
Matsukata Collection

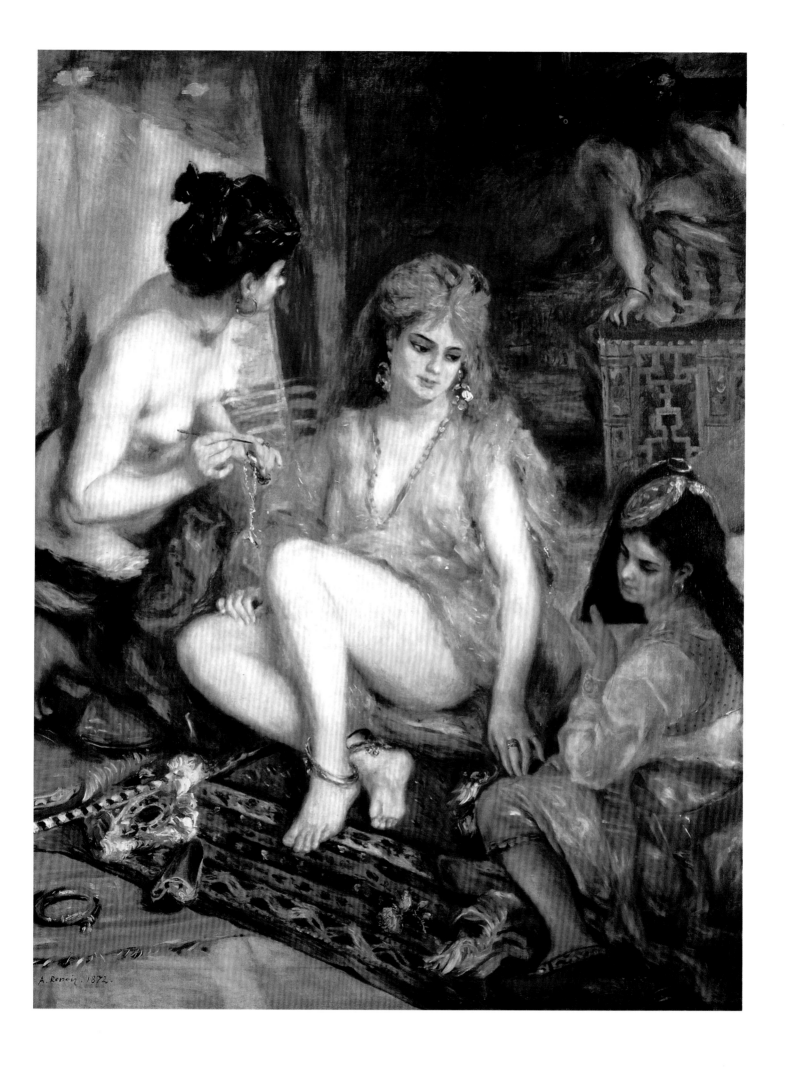

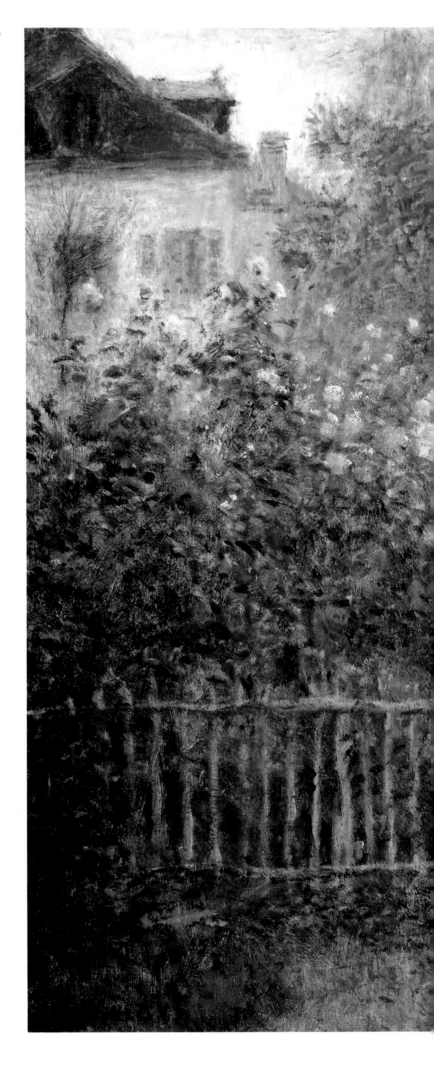

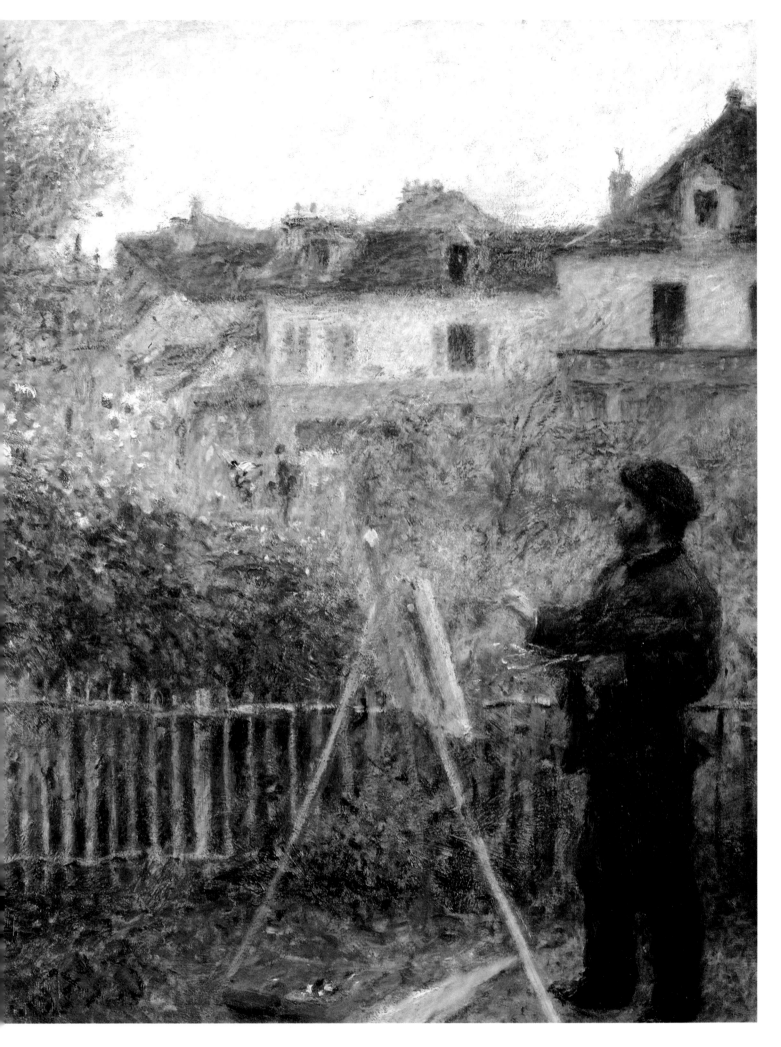

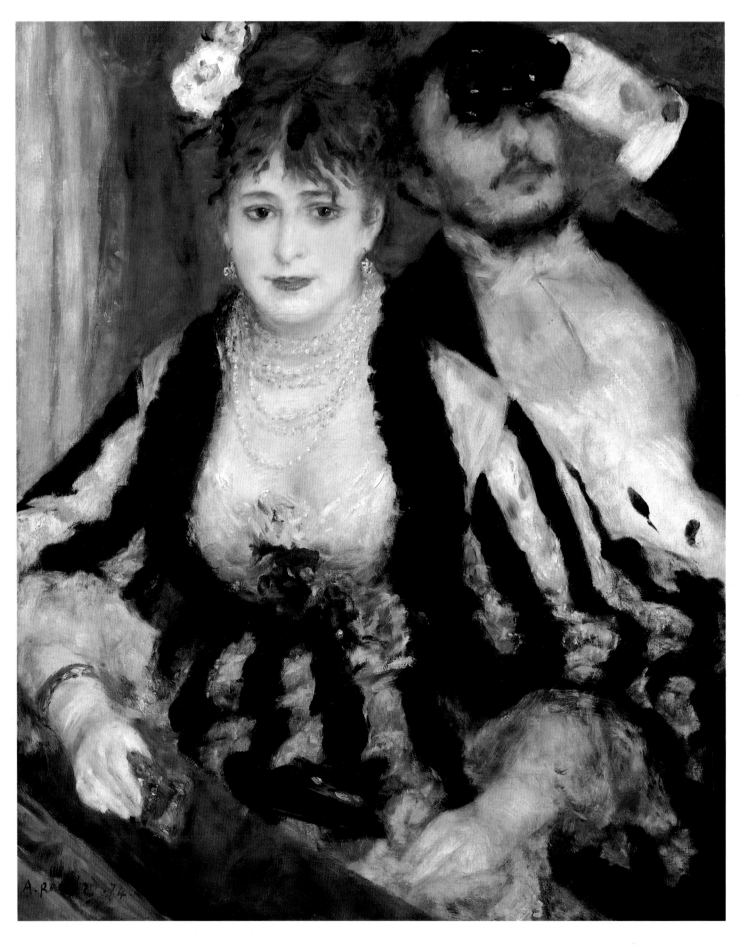

Above:
LA LOGE, 1874
Oil on canvas, 31½×24¾ inches (80×63 cm)
Courtauld Institute Galleries, London,
Courtauld Collection

Facing Page:
DANCER, 1874
Oil on canvas, 56⅛×37⅛ inches (142.5×94.5 cm)
National Gallery of Art, Washington DC,
Widener Collection

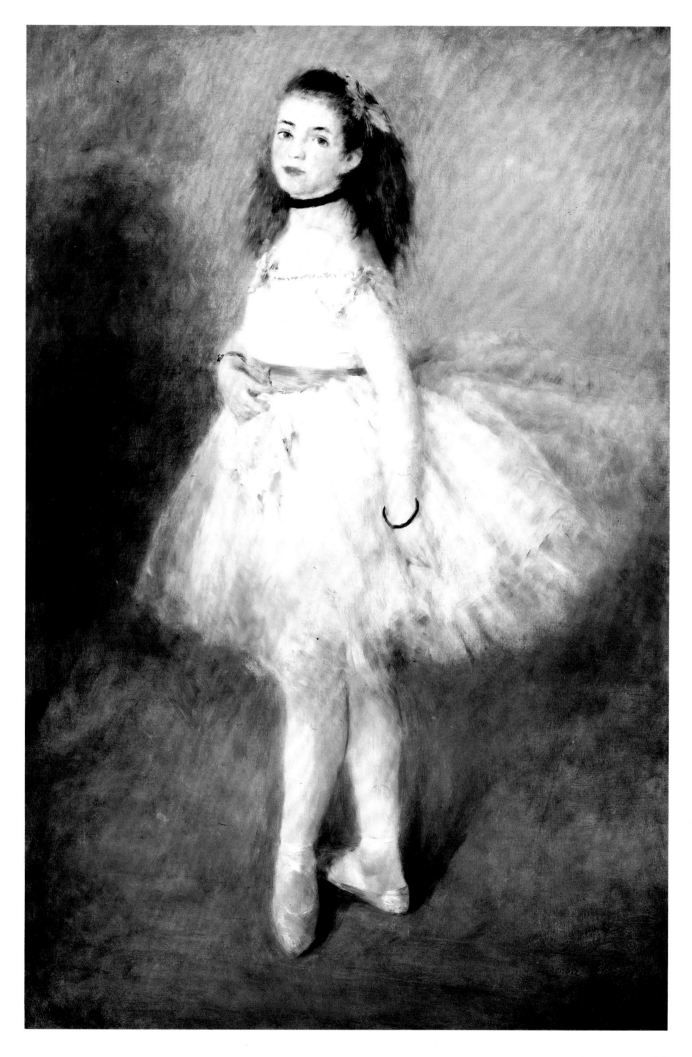

THE SEINE AT ARGENTEUIL, 1874
Oil on canvas,
19⅝×23⅝ inches
(50×60 cm)
Portland Art Museum, Portland, Oregon

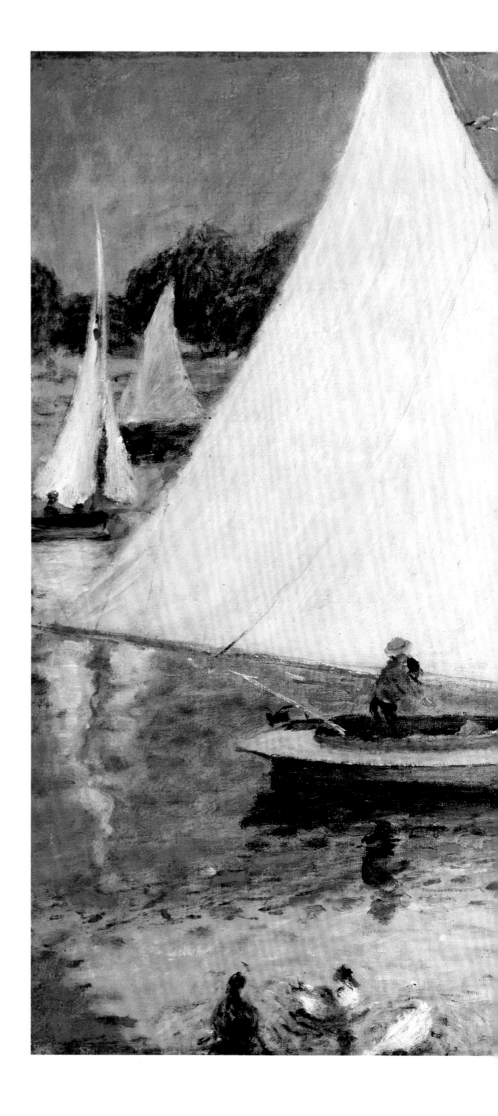

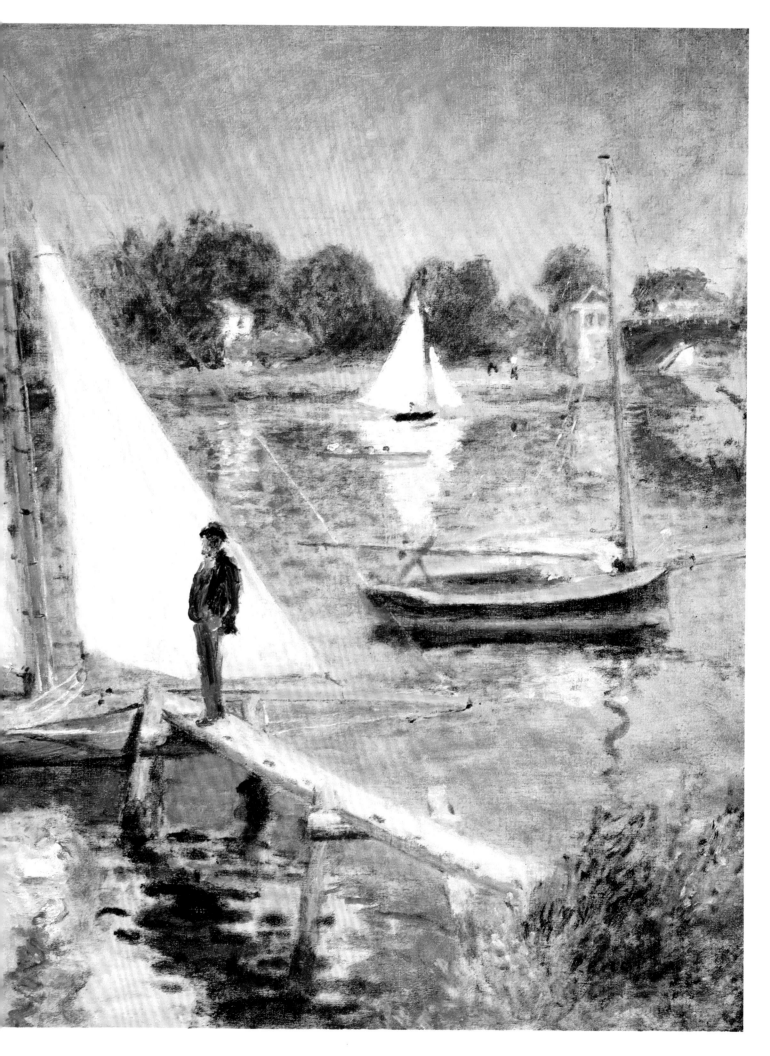

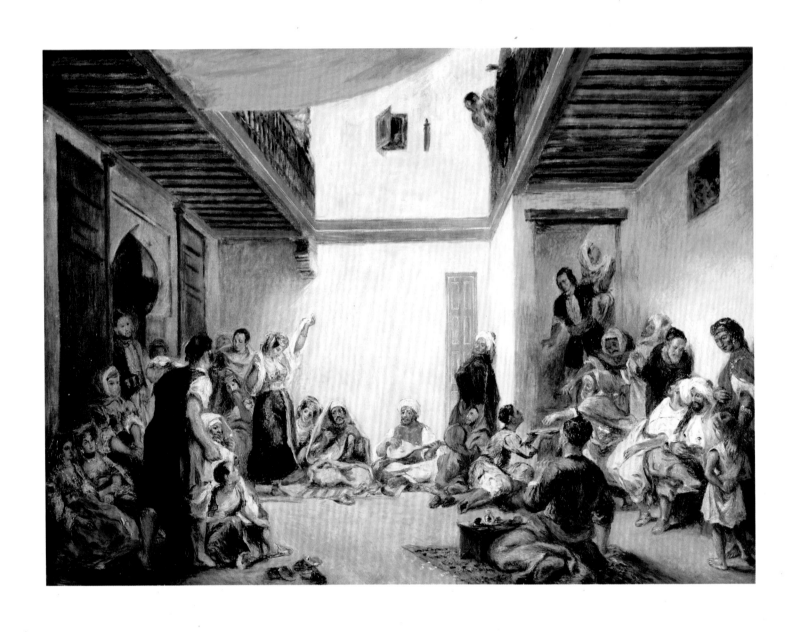

Copy of Delacroix's 'Jewish Wedding', 1875
Oil on canvas, 43×57 inches (109.2×144.8 cm)
Worcester Art Museum, Worcester, Massachusetts

28

PORTRAIT OF MADAME CHOCQUET, 1875
Oil on canvas, 29½×23⅝ inches (75×60 cm)
Staatsgalerie, Stuttgart

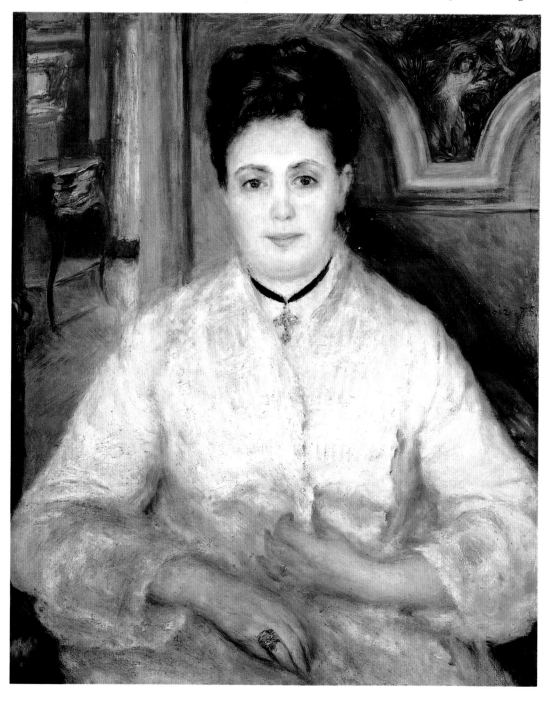

THE BALL AT THE MOULIN DE LA GALETTE,
1876
Oil on canvas,
51½×68⅞ inches (131×175 cm)
Musée de Orsay, Paris

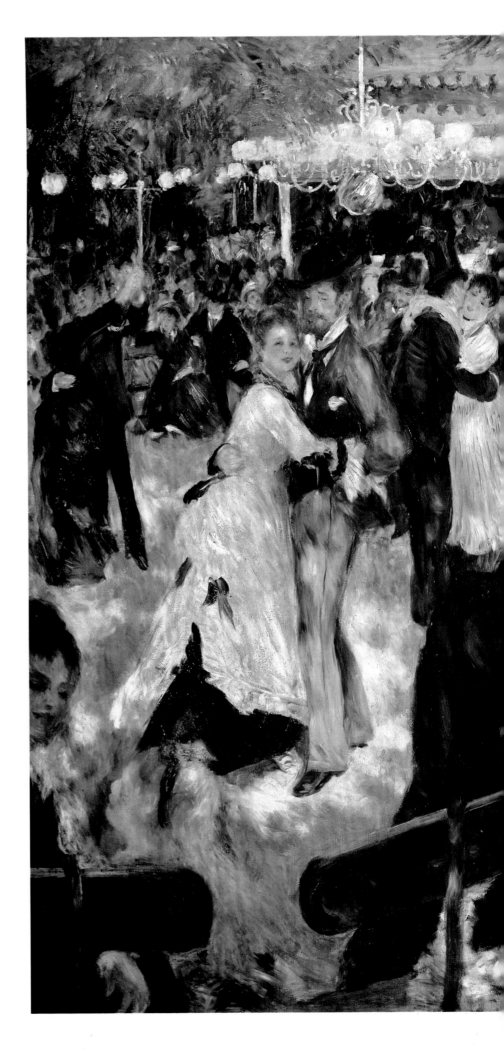

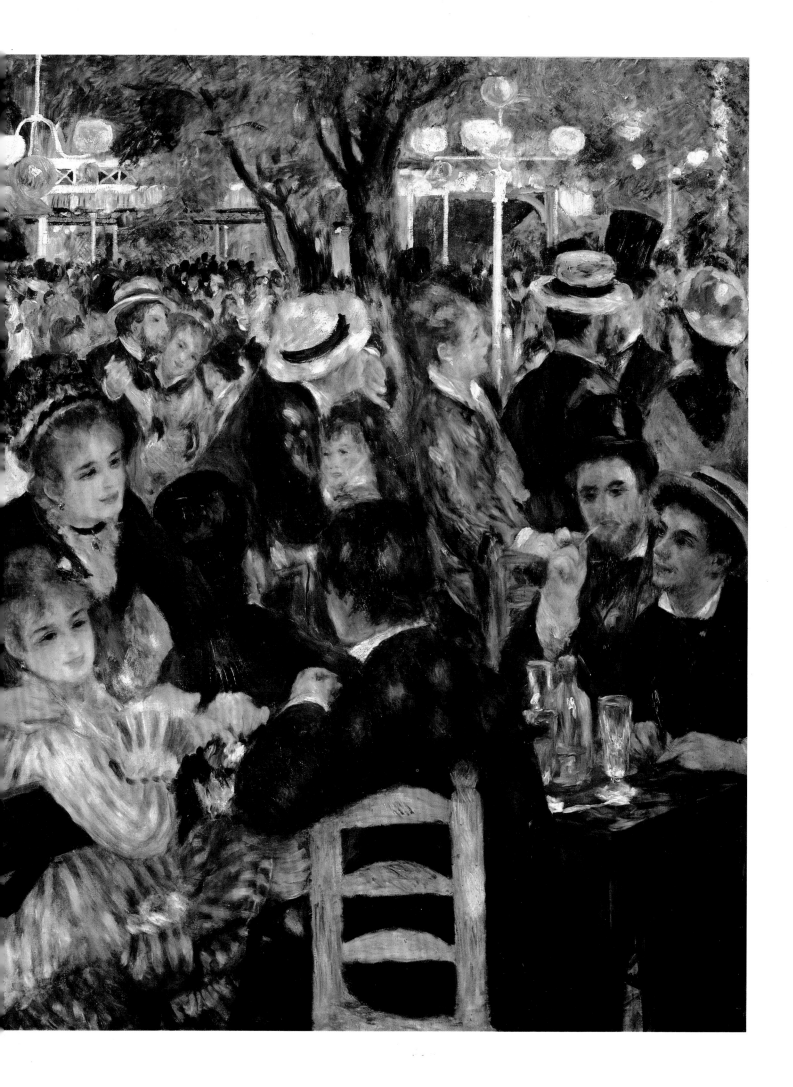

THE SKIFF, 1879
Oil on canvas, 28×36¼ inches (71×92 cm)
National Gallery, London

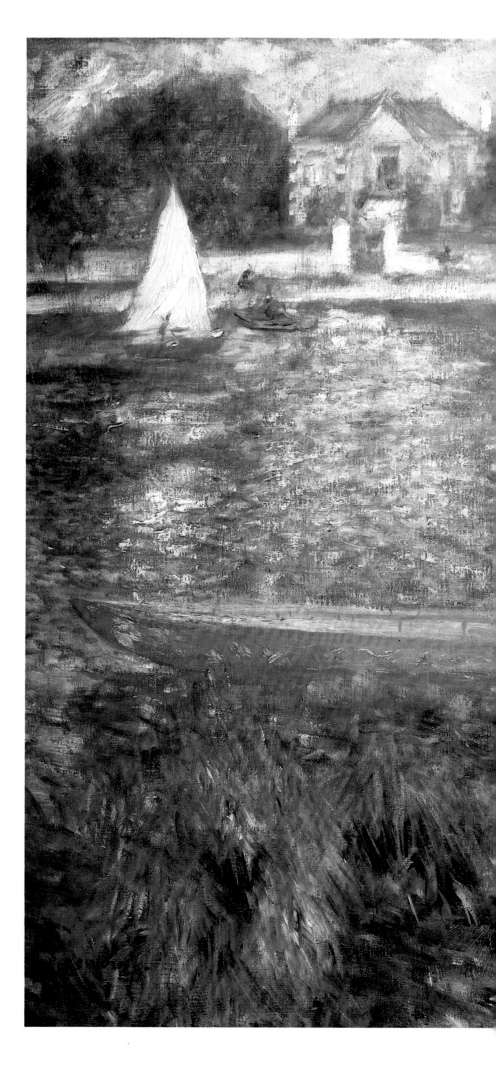

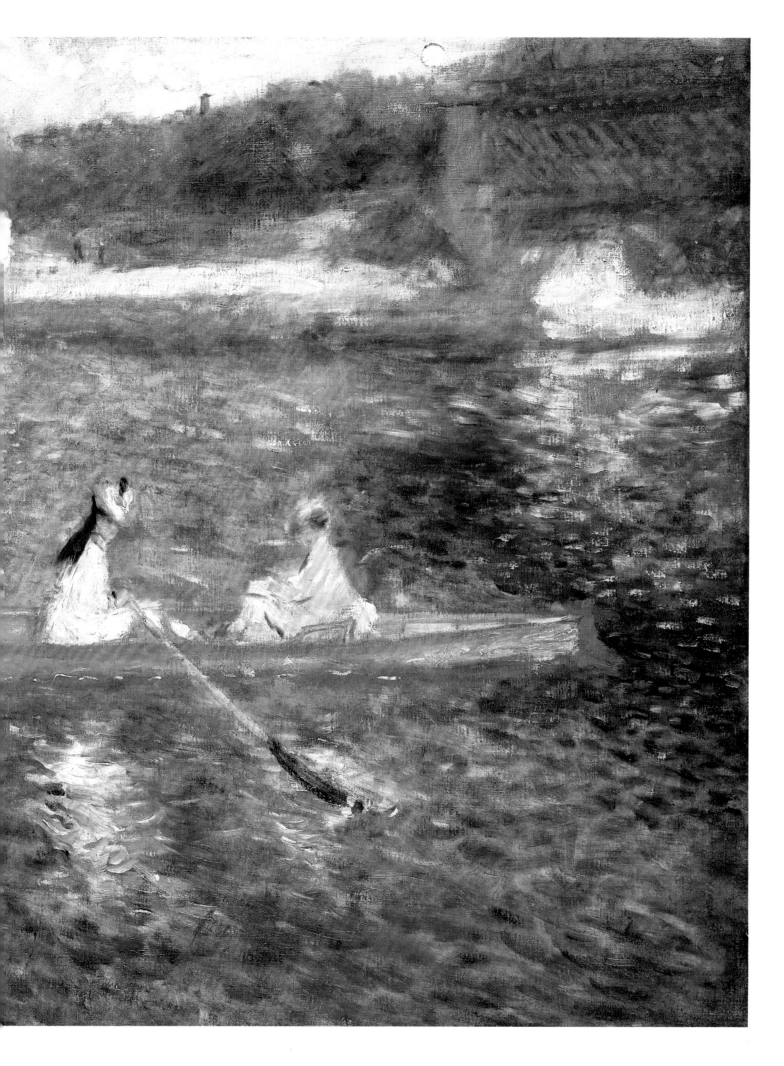

THE LUNCHEON OF THE BOATING PARTY, 1881
Oil on canvas, 51×68 inches (129.5×172.7 cm)
The Phillips Collection, Washington, DC

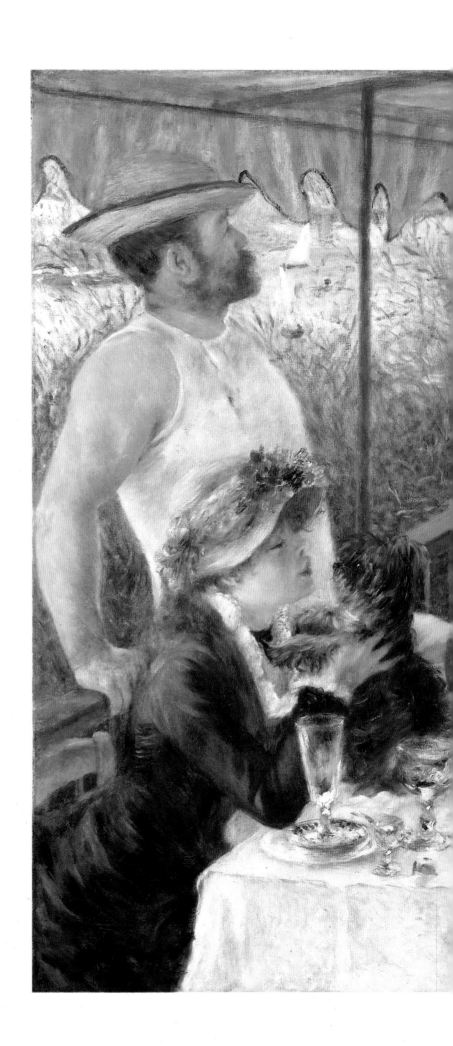

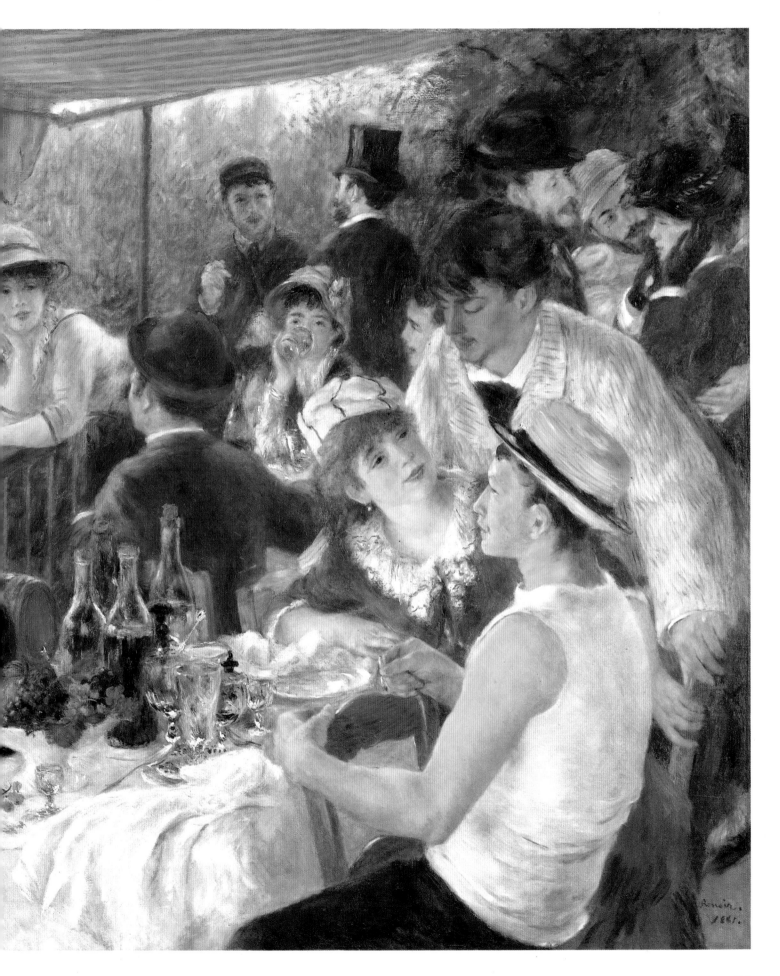

Venice: Piazza San Marco, 1881
Oil on canvas, 25¼×32 inches (65.4×81.3 cm)
The Minneapolis Institute of Arts
John R Van Derlip Fund

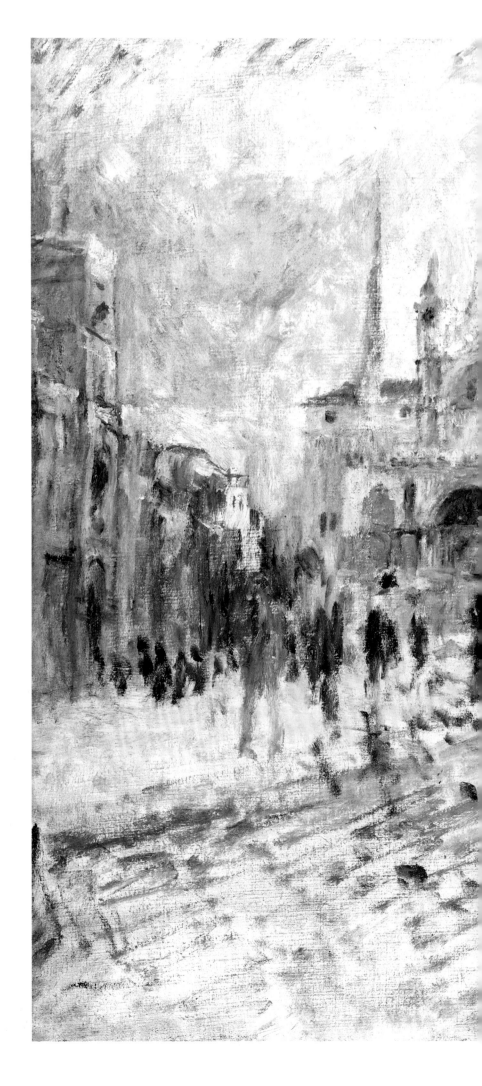

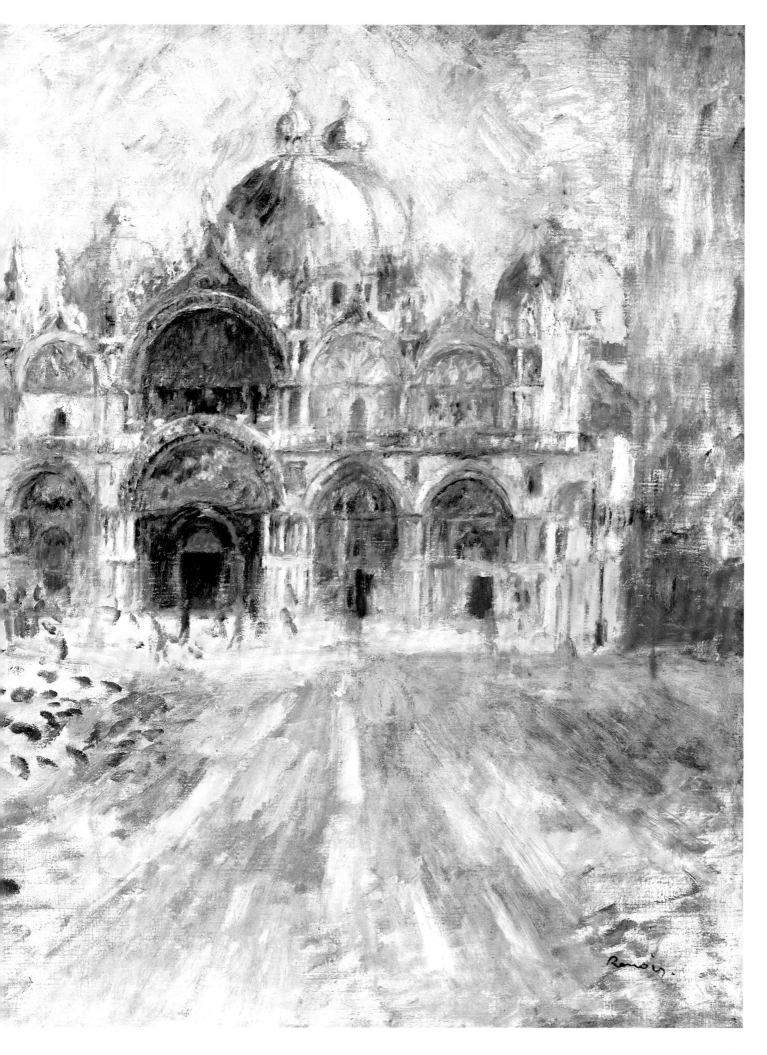

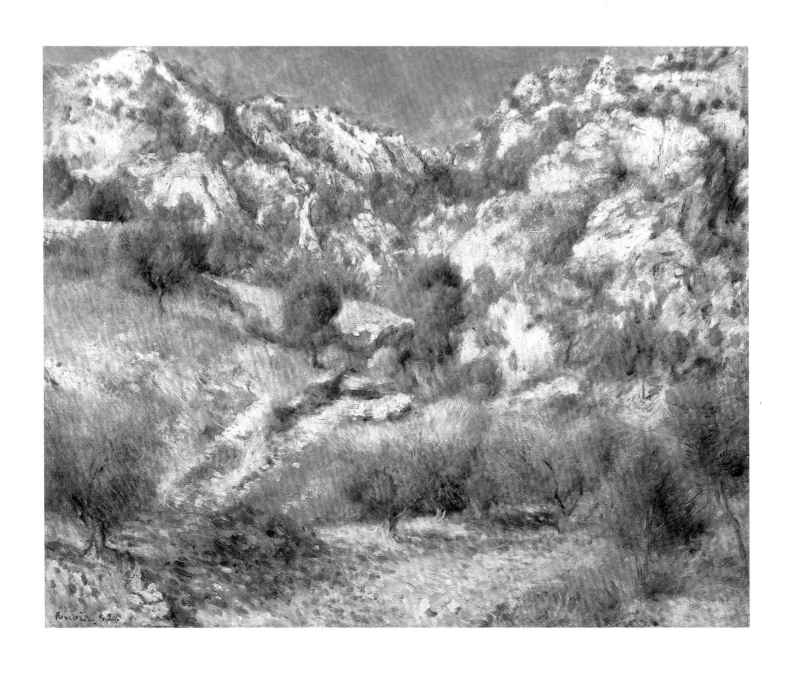

Above:
ROCKY CRAGS, L'ESTAQUE, 1882
Oil on canvas, 26⅛×37⅞ inches (66.5×81 cm)
Museum of Fine Arts, Boston,
Julia Cheney Edwards Collection

Right:
DANCE AT BOUGIVAL, 1883
Oil on canvas, 71½×38½ inches (182×98 cm)
Museum of Fine Arts, Boston, Picture Fund Purchase

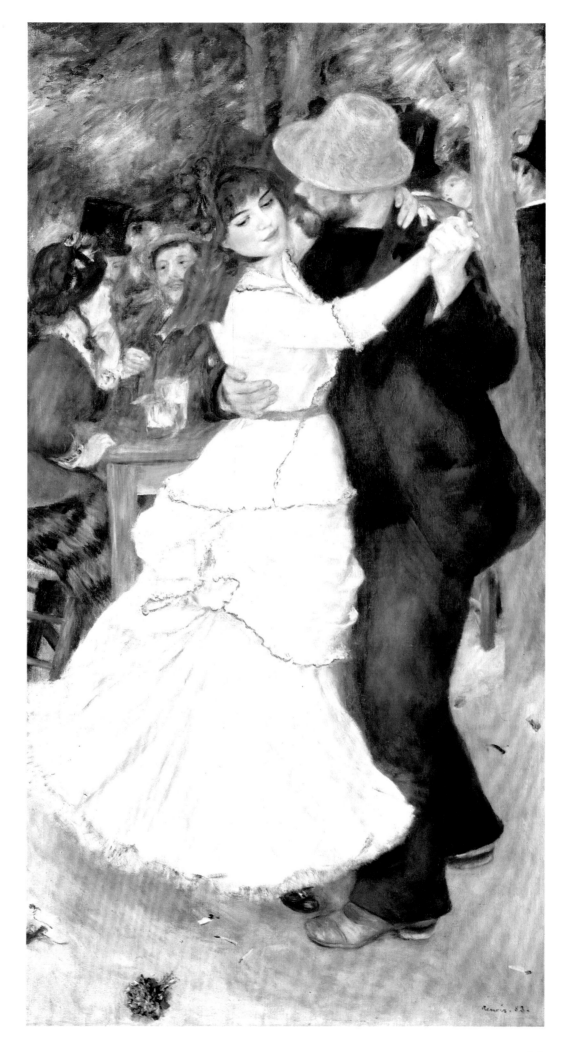

THE CHILDREN'S AFTERNOON AT
WARGEMONT, 1884
Oil on canvas, 56⅙×67 inches
(130×170 cm)
Nationalgalerie, Berlin

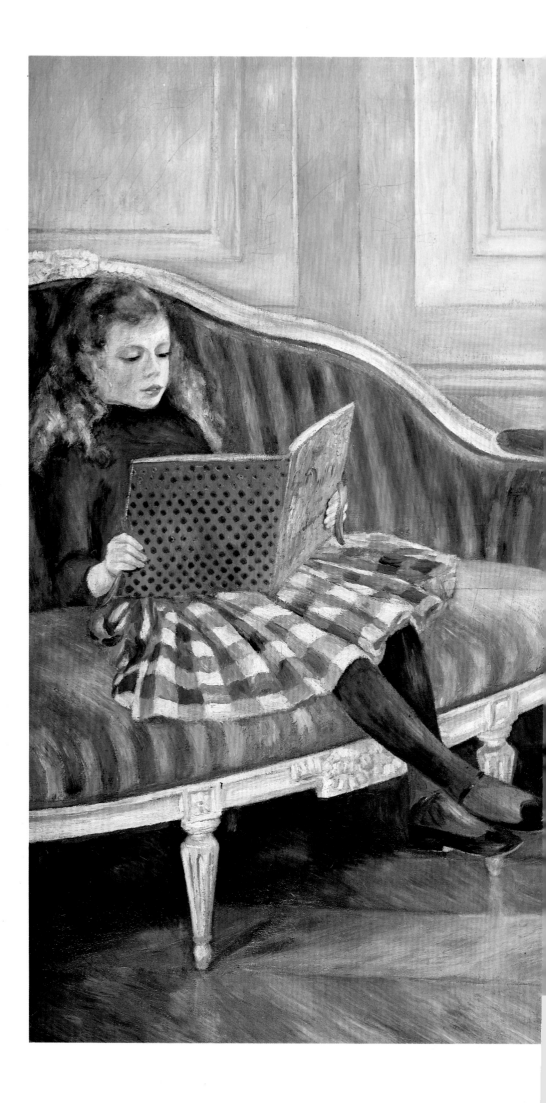

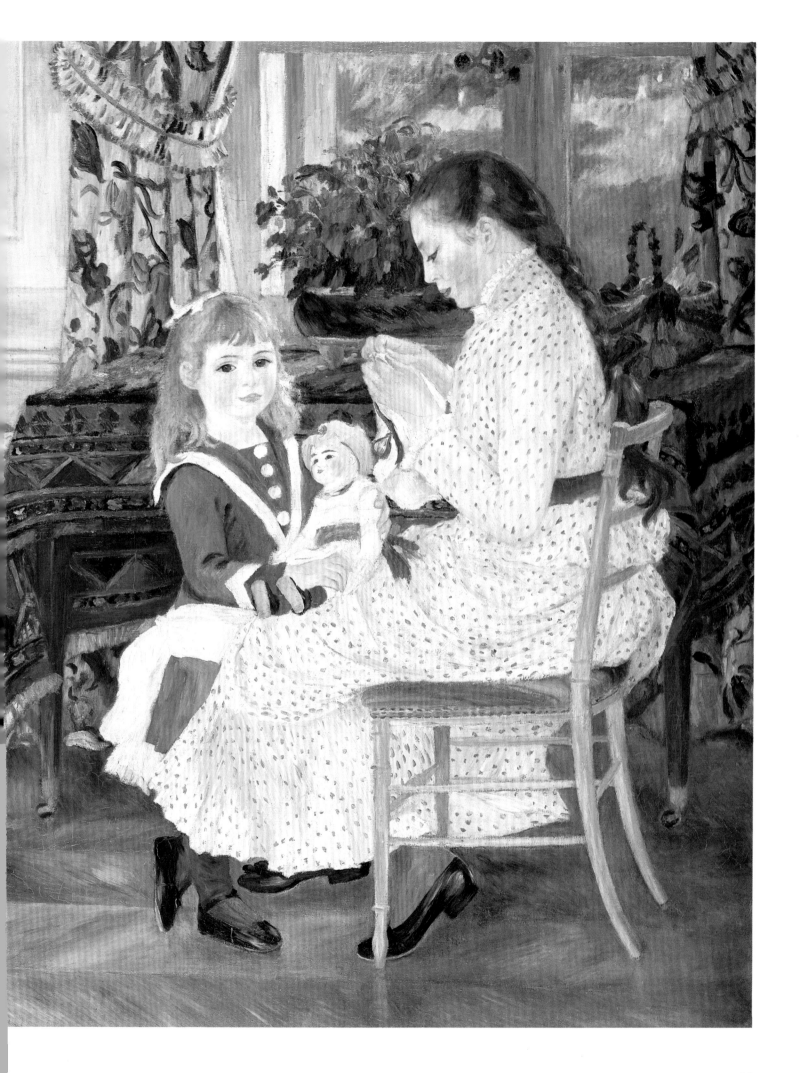

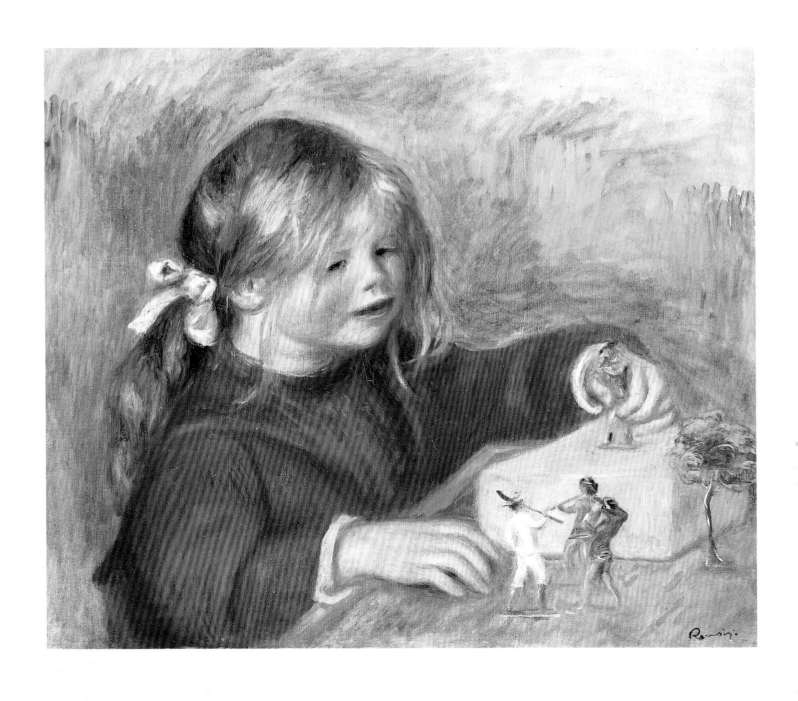

Above:
CLAUDE RENOIR PLAYING, c. 1905
Oil on canvas, 18⅛×22 inches (46×55 cm)
Musée de l'Orangerie, Paris

Facing Page:
THE UMBRELLAS, 1881-82, 1885-86
Oil on canvas, 70⅞×45¼ inches (180×115 cm)
The National Gallery, London

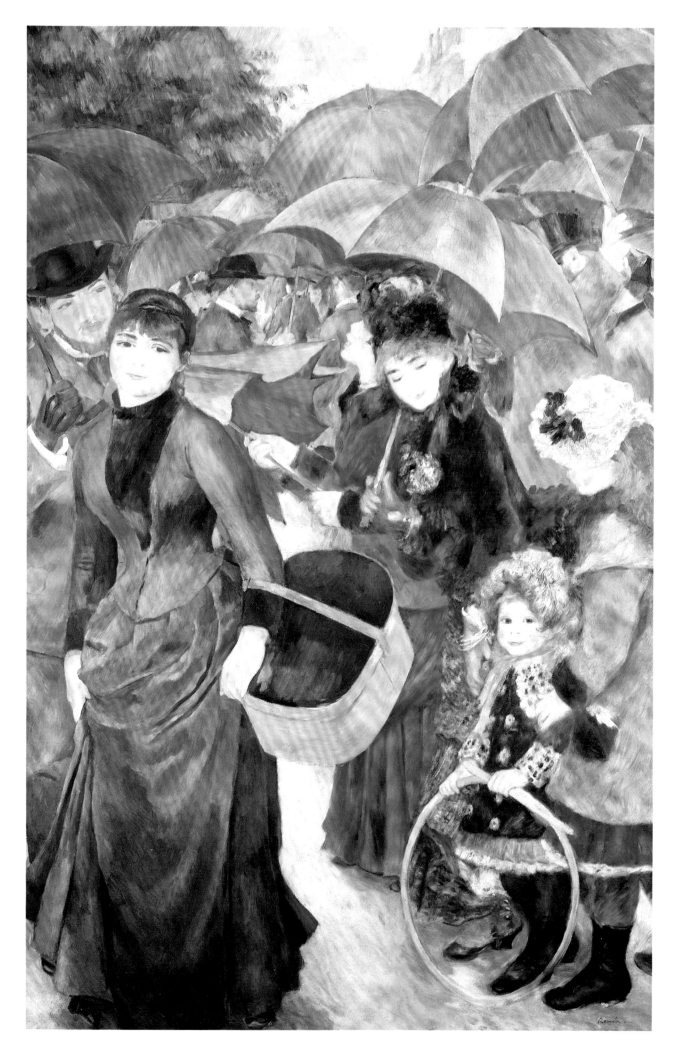

ACKNOWLEDGMENTS

The publisher would like to thank Martin Bristow who designed this book, and the following institutions for supplying the illustrations:

Courtauld Institute Galleries, London, Courtauld Collection: page 24

Folkwang Museum, Essen: page 4

The Minneapolis Institute of Arts: page 36 (John R Van Derlip Collection)

Musée Marmottan, Paris: page 20

Musée de l'Orangerie, Paris: pages 9, 42

Musée d'Orsay, Paris: pages 10, 30

Museum of Fine Arts, Boston: pages 38 (Julia Cheney Edwards Collection), 39 (Picture Fund Purchase)

Nationalgalerie, Berlin: page 40

National Gallery, London: page 14, 32, 43

National Gallery of Art, Washington DC: pages 18 (Chester Dale Collection), 25 (Widener Collection)

National Museum of Western Art, Tokyo: page 21 (Matsukata Collection)

Norton Simon Art Foundation, Pasadena, California: page 12

Oskar Reinhardt Collection 'Am Römerholz', Winterthur: page 11, 16

Phillips Collection, Washington DC: page 34

Portland Art Museum, Portland, Oregon: page 26

Staatsgalerie, Stuttgart: page 29

Wadsworth Atheneum, Hartford, Connecticut: page 22 (Bequest of Anne Parrish Titzell)

Worcester Art Museum, Worcester, Massachusetts: page 28